Jack's

Written by Georgina Green

Illustrated by Maarten Lenoir

RISING STARS

Mum and Jack went to the pond.

Jack hid his velvet fox in his backpack.

The velvet fox sits on a twig.

The fox tips into the vest.

The vest sets off!

Mum swims to get the fox.
They are wet!

The velvet fox is back!

My fox had a swim as well!

No fox on the next visit to the pond!

Talk about the story

Ask your child these questions:

1 Where did Mum and Jack go to swim?

2 What did the velvet fox tip into?

3 Who rescued the fox?

4 Do you think Mum knew Jack had taken his fox to the pond?

5 Can you think of another place you could go to swim?

6 Do you like to go swimming? Why?

Can your child retell the story in their own words?